Meditation Through Poetry

Meditation Through Poetry

2nd edition

Embark on a journey, with mindful poems for self-reflection and inner peace

Nikita Thakrar

Pesky Publishing Ltd

Copyright © 2024 Nikita Thakrar and Pesky Publishing Ltd

All rights reserved. No part of this publication may be reproduced, stored or transmitted in any form or by any means, electronic, mechanical, photocopying, recording, scanning, or otherwise without written permission from the publisher. It is illegal to copy this book, post it to a website, or distribute it by any other means without permission.

Cover image by Anthony via pixels.com, uploaded 04/08/2016 titled empty-forest-132428. Rights retained by Anthony.

Editions 1st (2024)

ISBN 978-1-7396901-8-2

Published by Pesky Publishing Ltd

https://journeywithnikita.com
https://meditationthroughpoetry.com

FOREWORD
by *Danuta Balcerowska*

Nikita has from an early age, been an intuitive observer of life. When you embark on a journey with Nikita, you walk a path towards self-discovery. Twenty years ago, the Dancing Nikita Company (DNC) was born; promoting Kathak, a classical Indian dance form and I was honoured to be her very first student. Since then, individuals of all ages and cultures have gained knowledge of dance but also personal confidence and motivation to achieve in life, through her holistic range of modalities for health, wellbeing and personal development.

Nikita's poetry is both an expression of her life experiences and an insight into the depths of her mind, heart and soul. The following poem is a tribute to Nikita for instilling in others, to never give up on your dreams and to always have faith in yourself.

In the cold darkness of winter,
a tiny seed patiently awaits the warmth of spring, kindness to breathe hope
into the life-force within.
Tentatively an idea grows into the light-seeking bud of promise,
nurtured into bloom by summer's gentle rain.
Tenacious of life no scorching
comment or frosty look can destroy the will to thrive and
blossom from within.

Danuta Balcerowska

DEDICATION

This book is dedicated to anyone who has ever had a vision. I hope it inspires you to not only follow your dreams but also pursue your passion and purpose.

ACKNOWLEDGMENTS

Thank you to everyone who has ever believed in me, particularly my parents, husband and members of my dance school who have supported my goals and dreams.

INTRODUCTION

***Meditation through Poetry* is designed to take readers on an inward journey of self-reflection.**

Exploring universal themes of birth, death and life itself, each poem is aimed to provide the reader with moments of mindfulness and to develop self-awareness.

The author's interpretation allows scope for further understanding from the poet's perspective.

The reader's reflections are encouraged to be used as journaling prompts for introspection.

Due to the complexities of human emotions explored in this book, while some poems may resonate deeply with readers, others may touch upon sensitive subjects that might evoke strong feelings.

Writing can be a cathartic process if done with intention and mindfulness. I hope that this book provides you with inner peace so that you can reflect on your own journey through life.

Nikita

Journey with Nikita

CONTENTS

INTRODUCTION 9
CONTENTS 11
MEDITATION 13
BIRTH 16
THE MOUNTAIN OF LIFE 19
FIGHT FOR YOUR DREAM 22
GOING HOME 25
MUSIC 29
SORRY THAT I WAS BORN 31
DANCE 33
DANCED THROUGH THE AGES 35
WILL I EVER DANCE AGAIN? 38
A WOMAN'S STRENGTH 39
IT WAS ALL A DREAM 41
THE WAITING GAME 45
WHERE ARE YOU? 48
POETRY 49
YOU CAN'T. 50
RELIGION 53
MAYA 56
THE VOICE INSIDE 59
SOULMATE 61
WHEN WILL THAT DAY COME? 62
WAITING FOR A CHANCE 65

IN MY NEXT LIFE 66
MY PURPOSE... 68
ABOUT THE AUTHOR... 71

MEDITATION

I sit still as I watch, my thoughts pass by,

Some fly past and others take time.

I am not getting involved in the play of my mind,

I remain detached and stillness I find.

Nothing remains, only my breath,

I am with the core of my being, my inner depth.

I hear it sing and feel it vibrate,

I connect with myself through a bond of faith.

My thoughts and desires have now disappeared,

As I swim in the pool of emptiness, nothing is to be feared.

Author's Interpretation:

This poem captures the experience of meditation, using vivid imagery and sensory details to describe the process of connecting with oneself.

The poem opens with a powerful metaphor, comparing our flow of thoughts to objects passing us by. This creates a sense of detachment and introduces the idea that we are separate from our minds.

As the focus shifts towards the breath, it becomes the only remaining element once the mind becomes quiet.

The phrase "core of my being" refers to a sense of vibration and inner knowing that can only be achieved through a deep state of silence and stillness.

The dissolution of thoughts encourages the disappearance of desires, creating a sense of harmony and peace. The emptiness is described as a "pool" where we can swim with freedom once we are no longer bound by our racing minds.

Reader Reflection Prompts:

How does the imagery of thoughts "passing by" resonate with your own experience of meditation?

Have you ever experienced a connection with your "core of being"? If so, how would you describe it?

Does the concept of "emptiness" evoke fear or peace for you?

BIRTH

As I look down below, and watch them conceive,

I prepare to be born; from the soul realm, I shall leave.

I will come into their world, to bring a ray of hope,

With happiness and joy, for my new parents to invoke.

Nine months in the womb, for my body to grow,

Into a life-size baby, for my new family to show.

I feel no suffering or pain, despite what I cause,

When I enter the world, I receive a welcoming applause.

The first moments I breathe, I continue to cry,

Until I open my eyes; I am greeted with pride.

Wrapped up warm, protected and loved,

My innocence is pure, I am not made to feel judged.

These are the best moments of my life, my soul can now express,

For the rest of my time on Earth, until I depart through death.

Author's Interpretation:

The poem 'Birth' takes a unique perspective, exploring the abstract experience from the viewpoint of an unborn child.

The poem opens with the soul observing and preparing for their own birth, suggesting a degree of awareness before entering the physical world.

The child expresses a desire to bring hope and happiness to their new parents, whilst acknowledging the gestation period as a time for the soul to grow and prepare for life outside the womb.

Drawing on the innocence of a newborn and the miracle of birth, as the beginning of the soul's journey of expression on Earth.

Reader Reflection Prompts:

What aspects of your own birth story or giving birth do you remember or cherish?

THE MOUNTAIN OF LIFE

Life is like a mountain, we all have to climb,

Sometimes we wish it would end,

but it takes its own sweet time.

Things may be going smooth,

and you have no worries at all,

Then along comes a bumpy path,

you may have a great big fall.

You see that others are ahead of you,

and you feel left behind,

Everything is going wrong;

the mountain is much too high.

You have your ups and downs,

and feel the highs and lows,

You think the mountain you are climbing,

is going much too slow.

By the time you have reached to the top,

You are tired and out of breath.

You have seen everything that life has to offer you,

And now is the time to rest.

Author's Interpretation:
This poem uses a powerful metaphor of a mountain to depict the challenges and triumphs that we all encounter through life.

It highlights the seemingly endless journey, acknowledging the time and perseverance required throughout our struggles.

The poem describes contrasting paths, through varying periods of smooth sailing along with "bumpy paths" and potential falls, representing life's unpredictable nature.

It explores feelings of being behind or overwhelmed by the challenges thrown our way, that can feel discouraging at times.

Reaching the peak of the mountain symbolises the culmination of life's experiences and the elimination of one's desires.

The poem acknowledges fatigue of the journey but also suggests a sense of accomplishment upon completion, embracing the opportunity to pause and rest.

Reader Reflection Prompts:

How does the metaphor of life as a mountain resonate with your own experiences?

What are some of the "bumpy paths" you've encountered on your climb?

What are the "peaks" or moments of fulfilment you've experienced?

FIGHT FOR YOUR DREAM

When you are striving towards a dream,

It doesn't happen, as it may seem,

There are times when you feel, like you have to fight,

Until your dream, is somewhere in sight.

You may need to beg, you might need to plead,

For your hopes and dreams, are the only thing that you need.

Never give up, not even for an hour,

Always keep hold, of your strength and power.

Never weep, with hopeless tears,

Never worry, about your fears.

No matter what, people say,

Your desires and dreams will never go away.

Author's Interpretation:

This poem is a call to action, urging readers to persevere in pursuit of their dreams. Acknowledging that achieving dreams requires effort and persistence, shattering the illusion of instant success. It emphasises the ongoing struggle required to navigate towards one's aspirations.

The poem also stresses the importance of a strong desire and unwavering focus on the dream itself. Hope is depicted as an anchor for the crucial lifeline that sustains the dreamer during moments of doubt.

Persistence and strength are encouraged for continual effort, holding onto hope and resilience, and avoiding giving up. The poem encourages the reader to confront and manage fear instead of dwelling on circumstances which are beyond control. Despite external challenges, the poem highlights the importance of inner strength, and the power that dreams and desires hold within oneself.

Reader Reflection Prompts:

What desires and goals are you currently pursuing?

Do you ever feel as though you are fighting for your dreams?

How can you cultivate unwavering hope and resilience in your journey?

GOING HOME

The time is now approaching,
As it is coming near,
I know that I am departing,
Yet I have no fear.

I am being summoned,
With a message from above,
It is not a call or order,
More an embracing of love.

To my dearest close ones,
I wish them goodbye,
They cry helplessly,
When I declare I will die.

They think I am giving up,
Unaware it is my time,
We all have to leave one day,
Now that turn is mine.
I get flashbacks of my life,
Playing on a timeline,
A rollercoaster of memories,
As I dwell on hindsight.

Nothing can be done,
No one can save me now.

As I approach death's door,
Not knowing when or how.

My heart still beats,
As I peacefully close my eyes,
My soul leaves my body,
And to my surprise.

I freely fly away,
Into the distance unknown,
As a beautiful ray of light,
Welcomes me home.

Author's Interpretation:

This poem explores the theme of death with acceptance and peace, acknowledging that death is a universal experience that everyone will experience. The poem portrays a peaceful passing, where the soul's separation from the body signifies the transition beyond the physical realm, leading to a state of liberation as they enter a peaceful and unknown destination referred to as "home."

Reader Reflection Prompts:

What emotions did this poem bring up for you, in relation to death?

Does the concept of a peaceful and accepting transition resonate with you?

Has this poem changed your perspective about death in any way?

MUSIC

Musical notes and melodies

Flow through the lyrics of rhyme,

Influencing emotions and moods,

Depending on the genre and time.

The bass in the background,

Supporting the instruments and tune,

The subtle power of music,

Can heal any pain or wound.

Reader Reflection Prompts:

What kind of music has a profound impact on your emotions?

Describe a specific time when music helped you heal or feel better.

Share your thoughts on the power of music to bring people together or create a sense of community.

SORRY THAT I WAS BORN

Sorry that I was born, if I got in the way

Sorry for being me, for wanting to play

Sorry if I was loud, or if my light was bright

Sorry for speaking my truth, for putting up a fight

Sorry that I was different, that I stood out from the crowd

Sorry I caused trouble, if I couldn't make you proud

Sorry I followed my dream, and went against the norm

Sorry I lived my purpose, I'm sorry I was born.

Reader Reflection Prompts:

Have you ever felt like you had to apologise for who you are?

Why is it important to overcome the fear of rejection and disapproval, and embrace our individuality and authenticity?

Why may other people get triggered if you are living your purpose?

DANCE

Dance is what developed, my eye to see,

I was trapped before, but dance set me free,

Dance gave me beauty, it enhanced my smile

It lights up my eyes and makes me feel worthwhile,

Dance allowed me to listen, enabled me to feel,

The illusion of a dream yet everything so real,

Dance taught me values, it showed me how to give,

It is through dance that I learnt how to truly live

Dance is a journey, that takes a lifetime,

So much to explore, like a mountain to climb.

Once I explored my body, I focused on my mind ,

Incorporated emotions and then came the time

For my mind, body and spirit, to all coordinate,

To produce a beautiful magic,

A mindless state…

Author's Interpretation:
This poem 'Dance' explores the transformative power of mindful movement, describing how it can awaken the senses, emotions, and spirit. The poem suggests that dance allows us to "see" in a new way, metaphorically referring to a newfound awareness or perspective. This freedom through dance is emphasised.

Dance is depicted as a way to "listen" and "feel" on a deeper level, blurring the lines between dream and reality. Dance transcends physical movement and expresses the idea that dance is a way of truly living, a continuous journey of exploration.

The poem compares the journey of dance to climbing a mountain, using it as a metaphor signifying the vast amount to discover and learn, and the progression from physical exploration to a focus on the mind, emphasising the importance of the mind-body connection.

The poem highlights the incorporation of emotions, resulting in a harmonious synergy of mind, body, and spirit. The final line 'mindful state' describe a state of effortless flow and "mindless magic" achieved through this complete coordination.

DANCED THROUGH THE AGES

I have danced through the ages,

Danced for many lives.

I played many characters,

I have been many wives.

I danced for the kings,

Performed in the courts.

Entertained the masses,

And gained the rewards.

Now the time has come,

For me to dance for myself.

There is no one left to watch me,

I have had enough wealth.

I wish to dance for my soul,

Which I have forgot,

I need to dance for myself,

And only for my God.

Author's Interpretation:

This poem explores the theme of reincarnation and a soul yearning to reconnect with its essence. Reflecting on a long journey through multiple lifetimes, playing various roles and experiencing the highs and lows of societal expectations.

However, the focus is not on the details of those past lives, but rather on the disconnection from their soul's purpose.

The poem concludes with a hopeful desire to reconnect with their true self and dance for their soul. This suggests a potential journey of self-discovery, seeking a deeper connection with their inner being and a higher power.

Reader Reflection Prompts:

Do you ever wonder what roles you may have played in previous lives?

WILL I EVER DANCE AGAIN?

Will I ever dance again,

Will I fly across the stage,

Will anyone want be there to watch,

When I am released from my cage?

Will I light up when I perform,

Will I uplift and inspire,

Will I fulfil my potential,

Will I achieve my desire?

Will I hear the sound of claps,

Will I see the curtain raise?

Will the lights shine down on me,

Will I receive the audience's praise?

Will I ever dance again,

Will they announce my name,

Will I be set free,

Will things ever be the same?

A WOMAN'S STRENGTH

A woman's strength, is tested over time,

Through the challenges she faces,

Determines her wrongs and right.

Her ability to face,

Her power of letting go,

Her selfless affection,

Is not just for show.

She effortlessly goes beyond,

Her dutiful role,

Getting stronger by the day,

Strengthening her soul.

Reader Reflection Prompts:

Who is the most inspiring woman in your life and why?

IT WAS ALL A DREAM

I am trying to make it easier,

Easier for my heart,

Easier to understand,

How my dreams got torn apart.

Perhaps I shouldn't dream,

Or maybe it wasn't real

Perhaps it is meant to be like this,

Is this an imbalance of the wheel?

What I just don't understand,

Or what I can't seem to digest,

Is why this only happens to me,

And why not to all the rest?

Is it because I am cursed,

Or do I simply not deserve love,

Will my luck ever be reversed,

Or will it always be this tough?

I am looking for an answer,

I am looking deep inside,

If you know what I am going through,

Then please, can I confide?

My heart feels like a toy,

Played with and used,

My mind is asking questions,
And my body feels abused.

Author's Interpretation:

This poem tackles the emotional turmoil of shattered dreams, unfulfilled desires, and trying to cope with a broken dream. The poem questions whether holding onto dreams is worthwhile, wondering if they were ever truly real.

The poem grapples with the concept of fate or imbalance, searching for a reason why dreams fall apart and doubting an intense sense of unfairness, questioning why they alone experience such disappointment. The poem explores self-blame and doubt, even questioning the possibility of being cursed or undeserving of love, highlighting emotional pain.

Seeking answers and a chance to reverse misfortune, despite a sense of hopelessness. The poem expresses a yearning to confide in someone who can relate to the same experience. The final lines paint a vivid picture of the emotional and physical impact of this heartbreak, comparing the heart to a broken toy and the body feeling abused.

Reader Reflection Prompts:

Have you ever experienced a dream being shattered? How did you cope?

What are healthy ways we can learn to manage our expectations and navigate disappointment and unfairness?

How can we develop inner strength and resilience to bounce back from setbacks?

THE WAITING GAME

I feel like a lost cause, like a waste of space,
A wandering soul, excluded from the human race.
My body sits here, my mind wants to go,
My heart cries out, my face has no glow.
I keep my thoughts and feelings, locked up inside,
Only to express them when, I go away and hide,
I spend time by myself, wishing I could die,
There is nobody there for me, except the sound of my cry.
I long for my childhood, as teardrops tirelessly fall,
My emotions are out of control, my dignity is so small.
My soul feels trapped, I want to be set free,
A battle inside, can someone please save me.
I cry myself to sleep, I weep every night,
Bathing in my tears, washing away my fright.
I am tired and hurt, disinterested in life,
Awaiting the end, of this long, lonely strife.
All the pain and suffering, my hope brings me shame,
When will the day come, when I end this waiting game?

Author's Interpretation:

The poem 'The waiting game' delves into the depths of despair and loneliness, capturing the pain of feeling lost and unseen.

The poem opens with intense emotions of feeling lost, negative self-perception and a sense of worthlessness. The internal conflict indicates a disconnect between the body that remains and the mind that seeks escape. The absence of a "glow" symbolises a lack of hope or joy. Bottling up feelings highlights repressed emotions and isolation.

The poem reflects on the longing for childhood, a time often associated with less complexity and pain, but more yearning for innocence. The plea for help suggests being imprisoned by our own negative emotions and a trapped soul crying out for salvation. Tears become a source of temporary release at night, washing away fear but not solving the underlying pain. The disinterest in life and a desire for the "waiting game" to end – suggesting a longing for release to an unknown but presumably better outcome. Hope itself is seen as shameful, leading to the question of how long this struggle must be endured.

Reader Reflection Prompts:

Have you ever felt lost, unseen, or disconnected from the world?

Have you ever experienced similar feelings of despair and loneliness?

How did the poem make you feel? Did it resonate with your own experiences?

WHERE ARE YOU?

Where are you when I need you,

When my heart is full of tears,

When I am crying myself to sleep at night,

When my world is full of fears.

Where are you when I need you,

When I am all alone at night,

When I have got nobody to turn to,

Just a blurred vision of fright.

Where are you when I need you,

When I am all by myself,

When I have no love in my life,

When I desperately need your help.

Where are you when I need you,

When I am suffering in pain,

Sorrow and loneliness show up,

But you, you're gone again…

POETRY

Poetry is words put together in rhyme,

The meanings are metaphoric, which can change over time.

The structure of language is played with like a game,

The depth of expression never remains the same.

The poet conveys, through the play of words,

Weaving through emotions, usually via curves,

A poet can reach out and touch a reader's soul,

A flow of creativity and the poet is on a roll.

The reader interprets from their point of view,

They reflect and relate, to create a meaning which is new.

Some readers relate, and others don't,

It depends on the format, the language and tone.

I am here to convey words to express my soul,

To impart and inspire, to fulfil my life's goal…

YOU CAN'T...

I am a woman, not a girl

You can't play with me.

I am mature, yet I am young

You can't use me.

I am a person, not a glass

You can't break me.

I have a heart, not a stone

You can't fight me.

I am strong, not weak

You can't test me.

I am innocent, not naive

You can't fool me.

I am me, not you,

You can't be me.

Author's Interpretation:

This poem is a powerful declaration of self-worth and strength. The tone of demanding respect with bold statements, asserting identity of a woman and establishing boundaries. The use of metaphors (not a girl, not a glass, not a stone) represents strength and resistance to manipulation. The emotional vulnerability acknowledges emotional depth and capacity for love, yet asserts their inner strength and refuses to be defeated. The suggestion of innocence with discernment highlights awareness and the ability to navigate the world without being naive. The poem concludes with a powerful statement of self-ownership and unique identity of being distinct and irreplaceable.

Reader Reflection Prompts:

What does it mean to be strong and independent?

How can we set healthy boundaries in our relationships?

What makes you, you? How do you embrace your unique identity?

RELIGION

Religion gives humanity a way to divide,

Some misbelieve, yet others take pride,

Religion can cause dispute, even conflict and war,

Uniting people together, giving them something to live for.

Having faith brings hope, when it is sincere,

If followers misunderstand then ignorance can bring fear.

People who fight and kill, in the name of God

End up suffering themselves, their values get lost.

We must seek to understand and realise the truth,

Keep an open heart, as you find out what is right for you,

Everyone is entitled, to knowing who they are,

Where they have come from and how to go far.

Explore your inner light, allowing it to shine,

Once you have touched your core, you will experience the divine.

You will not need saints or scriptures; you will have a clear vision,

Your identity will be revealed and that will be your religion.

Author's Interpretation:

This poem explores the complex and multifaceted nature of religion, acknowledging both its potential for division and its capacity to bring hope and purpose.

The poem emphasises the personal nature of faith, encouraging each person to find their own path and the importance of self-exploration and embracing one's inner light.

The poem suggests that true religious experience comes from finding our divinity within, not from external sources like figures or scriptures.

Reader Reflection Prompts:

How can we promote interfaith, understanding and respect?

What does it mean to have a "personal spiritual journey"?

How can we connect with our inner selves and find meaning in life?

MAYA

There is a devil inside me,

Eating me away,

An uncontrollable force,

Leading me astray.

She enhances my vices,

Encourages me to do wrong,

A battle between good and bad,

A fight to be strong.

She tempts my senses towards evil,

Veils my sight to be blind,

Obstructs my spiritual growth, she influences my mind.

What is this powerful force,

Creating a destructible intrusion,

A force of dominant energy,

Which itself is an illusion.

I cannot let her prevail, if I want to go higher,

I need to take control, I need to conquer Maya.

Author's Interpretation:

This poem explores the concept of Maya, a term often used in Hinduism and Buddhism to represent illusion or delusion.

The poem opens with an internal conflict between our good and bad nature, painting a powerful image of a "devil within," It explores temptation and loss of control, along with vices and morality, emphasising the battle between good and bad within.

The use of sensory deception and spiritual hindrance makes us question the nature of this powerful force, acknowledging its destructive and illusory nature. The poem takes a determined turn of resolution, recognising the need to conquer and overcome delusion in order to achieve spiritual progress.

Reader Reflection Prompts:

What are some ways we can overcome temptations and internal struggles in our own lives?

How can we strengthen our willpower and make choices that align with our values?

How can we achieve spiritual growth and a sense of purpose in life?

THE VOICE INSIDE

When you are feeling low, sad or down,

Do not get affected, do not even frown,

To know what to do, you just have to find,

That deep inner voice, the voice inside.

We all experience both pain and pleasure,

Learning how to cope, is the greatest treasure,

Never have doubts, just let your faith ride,

Listen to your inner voice, the voice inside.

Find silence within and you will get all the answers,

Touch your deep inner self and realise your pure conscience,

The waves will be smooth, there will no longer be a tide,

Your inner voice will save you, the voice inside.

It is always there, it never goes away,

It is ready to guide you and show you the way.

So next time you need it, just confide,

In your wise inner voice, the voice inside…

Reader Reflection Prompts:

Have you ever experienced a situation where your inner voice helped you make a decision?

How can we create space for introspection and listen more intently to our intuition?

Can you think of a metaphor or image that represents your inner voice?

SOULMATE

Sometimes I find it hard,

Hard to express and say,

That I am grateful for your presence,

Grateful each and every day.

You make me laugh and smile,

In a different way to the rest.

Our bond is unique,

Making you the very best.

Despite our hard times,

If we disagree and row,

We make beautiful memories,

Which bind our eternal vow.

A lifetime of memories,

Have been shared with you.

The most exciting experiences,

The good times we have been through.

A bond so strong,

Should never have to end,

I pray you will always be, my soulmate and best friend.

WHEN WILL THAT DAY COME?

When will that day come, when the world will see,

When they recognise the talents and gifts within me.

I am waiting for a chance, that one ray of hope,

For someone to believe in me, to say yes and not no.

When will that day come, when I no longer need to try,

To express who I am, to fly as free as a kite.

I tirelessly wait, running out of time,

I need to live that moment; I want that chance to be mine.

When will that day come, when I will feel alive,

When I will not need to suffer or need to sacrifice.

Every one step closer, is still too many steps away,

Towards my ultimate dream, for that one special day.

When will that day come, when the world will need me,

Will it be too late by then, when will that day be?

Author's Interpretation:

This poem explores the yearning for recognition and opportunity. It expresses a desire to share one's talents and gifts, highlighting the importance of hope and external validation.

The poem describes a desire to achieve a sense of liberation, yet the need to seize the moment and claim opportunities. The longing for fulfilment describes a yearning to feel truly alive and free from suffering or sacrifice.

The contrast between the distance of the current state and the dream highlights the ongoing effort towards achieving it. The uncertainty suggests a fear of missing out or the dream arriving too late.

Reader Reflection Prompts:

Have you ever felt like your talents or abilities are unrecognised?

How can we overcome impatience and self-doubt and believe in ourselves whilst pursuing our goals?

What are some strategies for taking initiative and creating your own opportunities?

WAITING FOR A CHANCE

I am waiting for a chance,

For that one ray of hope,

For someone to believe in me,

To say yes and not no.

I eagerly wait, running out of time,

I need to live that moment,

I need that chance to be mine.

Every one step closer,

Is still too many steps away,

Towards my ultimate chance.

For that one special day.

IN MY NEXT LIFE

In my next life, I am going to live for me

I will not strive for success, or work hard to achieve

I am not going to write to inspire, speak to share

I will not teach to impart, even if my knowledge is rare

I am going to dance to my own music, sing my own melody,

I will be in a state of flow, with everything around me,

I am not going to sell my soul or share my heart,

In my next life I will love myself, each and every part

I will not try to make friends, people can come to me,

I will just be myself, in my next life I'll be set free.

Reader Reflection Prompts:

Have you ever felt pressure to achieve or conform to societal expectations?

What does self-love mean to you? How can we cultivate it?

Imagine you could create your ideal life. What would it look like?

MY PURPOSE

I want to be someone, I want to go somewhere,

I want to spread my knowledge; I have a desire to share.

The ideas are all there, the plans are in place,

I need to make it happen, need to run faster in this race.

I have been given a task, an important role,

I need to hold on tight, I cannot let go.

Even if things get tough, or if my vision gets lost,

I have to keep my faith going, keep going at any cost.

I have so much more to do, much more to achieve,

More tasks to complete, more rewards to receive.

My journey is still long, my aims are still high

I need to fulfil my purpose, until the day I die.

Reader Reflection Prompts:

Have you ever felt a sense of responsibility or duty towards a cause?

What does it mean to have a purpose in life? How can you discover yours?

Can you think of someone who inspires you with their dedication and purpose?

TESTIMONIALS

'It is truly evident that Nikita's 'Meditation through Poetry' has been crafted from a heart centered space. An equal journey of gentle soothing, balanced with anchorage in fierce pursuit of one's Dharma. This collection will make all your chakra's dance a little.'

- **Rebecca Lee (best-selling author)**

The poetry in this book is relatable and conveys the essence of what I have felt at many moments in my own life. The struggle, the self-doubt, the inner turmoil, the loneliness and the overcoming. The female voice comes through clearly and is powerful in a way that you know with certainty Nikita has felt deeply.

- **Julie Cunningham**

https://meditationthroughpoetry.com

ABOUT THE AUTHOR

Photograph by Sharan Rai

Nikita began writing poetry as a child and developed her passion throughout adulthood, as a tool for self-expression.

Following decades of soul-searching, Nikita culminates her spiritual knowledge, expertise, and vision of a world where we all live with passion and purpose.

Using poetry as a bridge, Nikita draws on her vast range of healing modalities, lived experiences and personal challenges, providing readers with an immersive experience as they embark on a holistic inward journey.

Meditation Through Poetry invites you to breathe deeply and find stillness within the storm. This book unveils how calming words can become a sanctuary for your mind, offering a gateway to introspection and a path to inner peace.

In a rapidly changing world, Nikita acts as a catalyst for purposeful progress. She aims to inspire and guide generations to explore their identity, through a rich toolkit of transformative modalities to discover, develop and design your Dharma.

Keep In Touch

To stay connected with me on social media, please scan the following QR code. I would love for you to reach out and share your feedback about this book.

 Find me on Instagram

@meditationthroughpoetry

Alternatively, find out more about Meditation Through Poetry here

https://meditationthroughpoetry.com

Or discover more about my wider work here

https://journeywithnikita.com

www.ingramcontent.com/pod-product-compliance
Lightning Source LLC
Chambersburg PA
CBHW061149170426
43209CB00035B/1951/J